MOVE AND GET HEALTHY!

GROW A GARDEN: SUSTAINABLE FOODS

WRITTEN BY
SUSAN TEMPLE KESSELRING

ILLUSTRATED BY
TATEVIK AVAKYAN

magic
wagon

Content Consultant:

Pamela Van Zyl York,
MPH, PhD, RD, LN

VISIT US AT WWW.ABDOPUBLISHING.COM

Published by Magic Wagon, a division of the ABDO Group, PO Box 398166, Minneapolis, MN 55439. Copyright © 2012 by Abdo Consulting Group, Inc. International copyrights reserved in all countries. All rights reserved. No part of this book may be reproduced in any form without written permission from the publisher.

Looking Glass Library™ is a trademark and logo of Magic Wagon.

Printed in the United States of America, North Mankato, Minnesota.
102011
012012

THIS BOOK CONTAINS AT LEAST 10% RECYCLED MATERIALS.

Text by Susan Temple Kesselring
Illustrations by Tatevik Avakyan
Edited by Melissa York
Series design and cover production by Emily Love
Interior production by Craig Hinton

Library of Congress Cataloging-in-Publication Data

Kesselring, Susan.
  Grow a garden : sustainable foods / by Susan Temple Kesselring ; illustrated by Tatevik Avakyan.
    p. cm. -- (Move and get healthy!)
  Includes index.
  ISBN 978-1-61641-861-8
  1. Vegetable gardening--Juvenile literature. I. Avakyan, Tatevik, 1983- ill. II. Title.
  SB324.K47 2012
  635--dc23
                              2011033083

TABLE OF CONTENTS

MILK

EAT TO GROW

Eating healthful foods helps you grow up strong! You need to eat foods made from grains, like whole grain rice, bread, or cereal. You need protein from foods such as meat, eggs, or fish. You also need dairy foods, such as milk, yogurt, or cheese.

Most of all, you need to eat fruits and vegetables. Fruits and vegetables come in all shapes, sizes, and colors. They taste great and give you important nutrients.

HOW MUCH TO EAT?

Divide your plate in half. About half of the plate should be vegetables and fruits. The other half should be foods made from grains and foods that have protein. You should have a dairy food like milk with your meal, too. This follows the US government's MyPlate guidelines.

6

SOIL SQUEEZE TEST

Do the squeeze test to find out what kind of soil you have. Dig down to where the soil is damp. Take a handful of soil and squeeze. Open your fingers. If the soil doesn't stick together, it has a lot of sand. If the soil stays in a ball, it has a lot of clay. If the soil crumbles a little, it is just right.

If your soil is not good, you and a grown-up can build a raised bed garden. A raised bed is like a big box on the ground. You build the box with wood or other materials and fill it with good soil.

Maybe you do not have a yard where you can plant. Find a sunny spot. It can be a deck, a patio, or a windowsill. Plant your fruits and veggies in pots or boxes.

COMMUNITY GARDENS

Some neighborhoods have community gardens. These are places where people from the neighborhood garden together. Ask a grown-up to check if your neighborhood has one. Or, ask your teacher to help you start a garden at your school.

WHAT TO PLANT

Talk with a grown-up about what to plant. You should plant veggies you know you like to eat. Try some new ones, too. Make a map of your garden space. Decide where each type of plant will go.

Lettuce, green beans, tomatoes, and onions are easy plants to grow. So, these are good plants to try in your first garden. You can grow fruit like strawberries in your garden, too.

HEALTHFUL LIVING

Gardening provides healthy food to eat. But gardening is also good exercise. Get sweaty while you pull weeds. Lift a shovel of soil and feel your muscles work.

Different plants need different amounts of space in a garden. Look at the backs of seed packets. They will tell you how much space that plant needs. Or ask a grown-up to help you check online.

Check what kind of weather is best for each plant. Some plants like to grow in cool weather. Others like it hot and sunny. Some plants grow quickly. Others take months before they produce fruit or veggies.

CLIMATE

Climate is the usual weather where you live. Some places are warm in April. Others are still snowy! Choose plants that will grow in your climate. Ask a worker at a garden store for suggestions.

Now you get to decide: plants or seeds? Many vegetables grow well from seeds. Others grow better if you start with a plant. Ask a worker at a garden store. He or she will know which is best for your garden.

It is easy to grow carrots, lettuce, and beans from seeds. Tomatoes, green peppers, and strawberries grow better if you buy the plant.

PLANTING YOUR GARDEN

Use your garden map to decide where to plant each seed or plant. Read the back of the seed packet. It will tell you how deep to plant each kind of seed and how far apart to space them.

Use a trowel to dig a little trench for your seeds. Drop the seeds in. Remember to space them far enough apart. Cover the seeds with soil and pat it down gently with the trowel.

Place plants on top of the dirt before you plant them. Then you can see how everything fits together.

Your plants need food to grow. If you are using potting soil, the food is already there. If your garden is in the ground, add food.

Plant food is called fertilizer. You can buy many kinds of fertilizer at a garden store. Read the directions on the package. Ask a grown-up to help you measure the fertilizer and add it to the soil.

COMPOST

Some people make their own fertilizer called compost. They collect vegetable scraps, grass clippings, and dead leaves. Together, these materials turn into compost after several months. Ask a grown-up for help if you want to make your own compost.

CARING FOR YOUR GARDEN

Water your newly planted seeds and plants. The seeds need to be kept moist. Usually you should water twice a week. Check the soil with your finger. If it is dry, give your plants a nice drink of water.

Your plant might droop if it needs water. But it might also droop if it is too wet. If your plant droops while the soil is wet, let it dry out for a few days.

WATCH THE WEATHER

If it rains, you do not have to water your plants. If it is very hot, you might have to water them more often.

Weeds will grow around your plants. You need to pull them out. Weeds block the sun. They take food and water from your plants. Pull out the weeds once a week so they do not get too big.

Watch for bugs eating your plants. Ask a grown-up to help you catch one. Take it to a garden store. The workers there will tell you what it is and how to get rid it.

WHAT IS AN ORGANIC GARDEN?

An organic garden is one that uses natural products to help it grow. Organic gardeners use compost or natural products to feed their plants and get rid of weeds and bugs. If you choose to grow an organic garden, ask a garden store worker for organic products.

Rabbits, deer, and birds also like vegetables and fruits. Planting gardens in raised beds or in containers can stop rabbits from eating your plants. Putting fences around your garden can stop the deer.

ENJOY YOUR VEGGIES!

Different veggies and fruits are ready to eat at different times. Your seed packets say when your plant will be ready. If you can't tell, taste it! If it's sweet and good, it's ready.

* Some fruits and vegetables change from green to another color when they are ready to eat. Tomatoes, pumpkins, and strawberries do this.

* Some just get bigger. Cucumbers, zucchini, peas, and beans are ready when they're big.

* Some come off the plant when they're ripe. Raspberries twist off the plant easily when they're ready.

* You can eat onions, lettuce, and carrots when they're tiny or wait until they get bigger.

EAT YOUR VEGGIES!

Eat lettuce uncooked in a salad or a sandwich. Have a grown-up cook onions in a stir-fry. Many veggies are good cooked or uncooked. Try green beans, peas, carrots, and tomatoes uncooked. Then try them cooked. Which way do you like better?

GET HEALTHY

1. Save up your money. Ask a grown-up if you can buy a bag of ladybugs at a garden store. Let the ladybugs loose in your garden. Ladybugs are good insects. They eat many plant-eating bugs. They will help your garden grow!

2. Grow tomatoes, onions, garlic, cilantro, and peppers and make your own salsa! Add any other veggies you like.

3. Grow herbs on your windowsill or in your garden. Herbs are tasty plants. They give cooked food more flavor. Get some small pots. Plant basil and dill seeds. Buy plants for rosemary, oregano, marjoram, parsley, mint, and thyme. Put them in a sunny spot and keep the soil moist.

4. What if you grow tons of green beans? You can't eat them all right away. With help from a grown-up, you can preserve the beans by freezing them. Then you can eat them in the middle of winter.

WORDS TO KNOW

cancer—any of a group of very harmful diseases that cause a body's cells to become unhealthy.

mineral—a substance found in rocks, the ground, and the food you eat. Some minerals are nutrients your body needs.

moist—just a little bit wet.

muscle—body tissue, or layers of cells, that helps the body move.

nutrients—the parts of food your body needs to live and grow.

preserve—to keep fresh for use later.

trench—a long cut in the ground that is not very deep.

trowel—a small, pointed shovel with a short handle.

vitamin—a nutrient your body needs that is found in different types of food.

LEARN MORE

BOOKS

Ehlert, Lois. *Growing Vegetable Soup*. New York, NY: Sandpiper, 1991.
Gibbons, Gail. From Seed to Plant. New York, NY: Holiday House, 1993.
McCorquodale, Elizabeth. *Kids in the Garden: Growing Plants for Food and Fun*. New York, NY: Black Dog Publishing, 2010.

WEB SITES

To learn more about gardening, visit ABDO Group online at **www.abdopublishing.com**. Web sites about gardening are featured on our Book Links page. These links are routinely monitored and updated to provide the most current information available.

INDEX